The Power of 1 Penny & 12 Questions

Gina Pomar

Published by Powerhouse, Inc.
Copyright © 2017 Gina Pomar

Printed in the United States of America

Pomar, Gina
The Power of 1 Penny & 12 Questions
Library of Congress Cataloging-in-Publication Data
ISBN-13: 9780999462102
ISBN-10: 0999462105
Library of Congress Control Number: 2017956594
Powerhouse, Inc., Murrieta, CA

Disclaimer

This book is designed to provide inspiration and motivation for overcoming adversity, embracing gratitude, and creating a life filled with positivity. It is sold with the understanding that the publisher and author are not engaged in rendering legal, accounting, or other professional services. If legal or other expert assistance is required, the services of a specialist should be sought. This text should be used only as a general guide and not as the ultimate source of information for the subjects discussed herein.

The purpose of this manual is to educate, motivate, and inspire. The author and publisher shall have neither liability nor responsibility to any person or entity with respect to any loss or damage caused, or alleged to have been caused, directly or indirectly, by the information contained in this book.

Contents

Introduction

I grew up asking questions. My Mom taught me to ask questions. One of our family mottos was, "You don't ask, you don't get!" You can imagine how excited I was when I found a unique-looking plaque with this exact saying on it while on a cruise in Mexico. I smiled, squealed and bought it!

My husband and I have been Success Coaches for many years. We coach and train **willing** people to succeed (emphasis on the word "willing"). If you want to succeed at anything in life, you must be willing to work, willing to do what matters most and willing to get out of your own way sometimes! A key to our success is asking great questions.

You know you've asked a great question when it is followed by a pause and beautiful silence. It means the person is thinking, processing, and possibly looking at their life in a new way. Questions help people self-discover.

We also like to use humor to keep people on the right track. We have a sign that says, "Yesterday was the deadline for all complaints." We don't want to hear complaints, we don't want to hear excuses. We want to see people focused on their goals, owning their mistakes, learning from them, and moving forward.

You can imagine how interesting it was for our two sons to grow up with two Success Coaches as parents! Our boys were easy targets and it came naturally for both of us to pepper them with questions to get them to think in new ways and not play the blame game of pointing fingers at others when things didn't go their way.

Great questions help us hold a mirror up to ourselves. This isn't a mirror of vanity to see if our hair looks good or if we have a huge chunk of cilantro in our teeth! The mirror I'm talking about is a mirror that reveals our true self.

Through the years we have found some people unwilling to take an honest look in the mirror. They don't want to see their true self. They want to hide behind complaining and blaming. Complaining about circumstances and blaming others.

We have seen people buck the mirror, not wanting to look in it, even when doing so would help them to help themselves and their relationships with others. Some people are not ready for the mirror and some may never be. It is sad to consider who they could become if they were willing to take even the slightest peek to begin their transformation.

Thankfully, we have also found people who are ready and willing to look in the "true self mirror". These are the ones that become the most successful. They are willing to answer powerful questions because deep down they want to be better. They refuse to play the blame and complain game.

They want to be real, and because of their willingness to be real, they are open to transformation. They are teachable and coachable. They do not pretend that they know it all. They are open to becoming the best version of themselves.

Are you willing to look in the "true self mirror"? The questions in this book are designed to help you do just that.

We've recently become empty nesters and we realized that we wanted our children to have powerful questions in front of them, always. Questions that empower them to be successful. Questions that help them to have a great relationship with themselves and with others. Questions that get them thinking, not just going through the motions of life. Questions that if they answer honestly, will empower them to take action and create amazing lives.

We decided to share 12 questions to empower our children and realized that these same questions could empower others as well (like you amazing readers). Hence, this book was born.

I believe that books and online classes can be short, sweet, and powerful. How many times have you read a book, loved it, and done nothing about it? I confess that I have done that more times than I can count! I was determined to write a book that readers could finish quickly and then do something about it. A book that would inspire and support action. This book is just that.

Each chapter contains one question that is brought to life through my own personal short stories. In these stories I share some of my struggles and some of my successes with overcoming obstacles, setting goals, losing weight, and finding my strengths. I share experiences about life, leadership, health, money, marriage, and parenting.

At the end of every chapter you'll find at least one blank page. This page is not a printing mistake. This page is there for you to use, if you choose. You can use this page to answer the question from the chapter or to write down any thoughts or feelings that you have about what you've read. If you don't feel like writing, you can just move onto the next chapter. The choice is yours.

Who is this book for?

- Teenagers
- Adults (at any age or stage in life)
- Couples (at any age or stage in life)
- Parents
- Families
- Coaches
- Teachers
- Trainers
- Leaders
- Business Owners

Remember that transforming your life is a process. Don't beat yourself up or be an overachiever, thinking you can transform overnight. (I'll be talking more about this in an upcoming chapter since I'm a recovering overachiever.)

Also remember that these questions can help you look in the "true self mirror" throughout your life.

Answering the same question next month or next year might bring a different answer, because you have become a different person. You have had different experiences. Experiences that have transformed you.

Enough already about questions. Are you ready to get started with the first one?

Chapter #1

Be Positive

Sometimes life throws us a curveball. A curveball we didn't see coming. A curveball that has consequences. We can't change the curveball, we can only change what we choose to do about it!

It was just another day in September and I was on my way to Gunderson High School in San Jose, California (a.k.a. Bay Area or Silicon Valley). I was 14 years old and sitting in the front passenger seat of a Bel Air. I didn't know that morning that something was about to happen to me that would change my life.

I didn't make it to school that day. I didn't make it back to school for weeks because I was in a serious car accident. We were driving through a construction zone and the sun was shining so brightly, it was almost blinding. A construction worker with a reflective vest suddenly jumped out to stop the traffic while waving a small flag. Unfortunately, the brake lights were not working on the car in front of us. It all happened so quickly that we slammed right into that car. I was not wearing my seat-belt and the impact of the collision threw me face first into the unforgiving steel dashboard. I was knocked unconscious and sustained traumatic injuries to my face and mouth.

The next thing I remember was being greeted by a kind stranger who stood next to my car. She was a nurse from a car nearby. I was still in shock and trying to wrap my teenage brain around what had just happened to me.

I didn't look in the car mirror to see my injuries. I think seeing myself would have sent me into more shock. I was not ready for the mirror at that moment. The nurse's face however was mirror enough for me. The look on her face told me that my injuries were severe.

I'm sure that I looked like someone in a horror movie except the blood on my clothes was real and it was on one of my favorite shirts! The blood never came out of that favorite shirt of mine. I ended up throwing my clothes away from the day of my accident. Sometimes it's good to hold onto things and other times it's good to let them go.

I don't know the name of the nurse who reached out to help me that day. I wish I did, because I would have sent her a handwritten thank you note. She didn't have to leave the safety of her car that morning to approach my car, not knowing what sort of trauma she would find there. She made a pro-active choice to offer her support in my time of need. She stayed with me until another sweet stranger arrived.

This stranger's face was positive and peaceful. His face told me that everything was going to be okay. He waited by my side and helped me remain calm until the ambulance arrived. I had heard ambulance sirens before, but never one that was coming for me.

I had emergency plastic and oral surgery the same day of the accident to repair the damage that had been done. I then began the long road to recovery. From one day to the next my world had changed, and I had some new realities to deal with.

One of those realities was that I was put on a liquid and soft food diet. That had its benefits since I could drink magnificent milkshakes and eat mounds of mashed potatoes. These were two foods I loved! That reality wasn't so bad after all.

Another reality was the fact that I had a fat lip. The kind that most people have if they get in a fight or take a fall, except they ice it and it goes away within a day or so. Mine didn't go away for months.

On top of the fat lip factor, I drooled. My bottom lip was extremely swollen and stuck so far out, that for a time, it didn't hold my saliva in. I got tired of dripping like a slow and leaky faucet and found some creative ways to stay positive and stay dry!

At the young age of 14 I had a choice to make. I had already struggled with self-confidence before the accident. I compared myself to others and didn't feel that I was all that great. The accident changed the way I looked and had the power to change the way I felt about myself, if I allowed it to.

I'm not going to lie, I had moments when I looked in the mirror and felt ugly and sad. I wondered if my fat lip and face would ever be normal again.

I threw some of my own pity parties. Have you ever hosted your own pity party? In time I learned to stop hosting them because I didn't like the way I felt at those parties. I wanted to get better and move on with my life. I ultimately had a choice to make.

I could choose to be bitter about my situation by focusing on my pain, my fat lip, and my inability to eat solid foods.

I could choose to hold a grudge and point the bitter finger of blame towards the driver of the car I was in, the construction worker who jumped out too quickly with the flag, or the person in the car in front of me whose brake lights weren't working. I could choose to be mad at the sun for shining too brightly that day and making it hard for the drivers to see!

or...

I could choose to be better by being positive and focusing on my blessings, like the huge rush of support from my family and friends following the accident. I could choose to focus on the amazing strangers who helped me through the accident like the calm firefighter who sat with me while I waited for the ambulance, the quirky but amazing plastic surgeon who talked politics while he stitched up my lip, and the incredible oral surgeon who cleared his schedule to perform emergency surgery on an insecure 14-year-old girl who desperately needed her teeth fixed so she could smile again.

I chose to be better! It felt so much better to put on what I call my "gratitude glasses" and look at life with gratitude for the many blessings I still enjoyed. I didn't know as a teenage girl the challenges I would encounter throughout my life, when I would need to grab those "gratitude glasses" again and again to keep looking for the positive. Those glasses would need to stay close by, not buried under my bed. Those glasses would help me continue to be better, not bitter!

Sometimes life throws us a curveball. We can't change the curveball, we can only change what we choose to do about it! When a curveball comes flying your way, you can do your best to remain calm and answer this important question. Are you choosing to be bitter or better?

Chapter #2

Be Aware

I was almost 16 years old when I met my husband, Miguel. I didn't know at the time that he would be my husband, but he says that the day he saw me across the crowded room at a church dance, he knew I would be his wife. His side of the story is fun to hear and perhaps he'll tell it someday in another book, but in this book, I'm going to share my side with you. Some people think we were high school sweethearts. I laugh out loud and tell them that we were more like a high school roller coaster!

The challenge was that Miguel wanted me to be his girl-friend and I wanted to be free. I had this obsession with keeping my options open. It wasn't that I didn't like him. I just wanted to be able to go out with whoever I wanted to. I didn't want to be tied down.

We spent a lot of time together and we have some hilarious 80's and 90's pictures to prove it. Our relationship was on again, off again, on again, off again, you get the picture. Most people who knew us said that we wouldn't last. If people had to choose a flavor of ice cream to describe our relationship, they would have chosen rocky road.

One of the things that kind of bugged me about Miguel was how nice he was. I know that sounds ridiculous, but it was true! He was so nice that he called me after the 1989 Loma Prieta earthquake to make sure that my family and I were okay. The earthquake was so massive that school was cancelled the following day. I assured him that my family and I were fine, but I was thinking, "Who is this guy? Why is he so nice?"

After high school graduation, Miguel left the country for two years to serve a mission for our church in Bogota, Colombia and I headed off to college. You would think that in those two years I would have figured out my feelings for him, right? Wrong! I faithfully wrote him letters and sent him packages but kept my options open. I dated several guys and ended up dating one young man exclusively for quite some time. Let's call him "Sean" to protect the innocent.

Have you ever been interviewed in your sleep? I totally talk and laugh in my sleep, or so people tell me! When I was dating Sean, my college roommate interviewed me in my sleep and told me about it later. She asked me two simple questions. 1) Do you love Sean? My answer was "no". 2) Do you love Miguel? Would you like to guess my answer? It was "yes". Apparently, my subconscious mind knew I loved him, but my conscious mind still needed convincing!

Several months before Miguel returned home, Sean proposed to me. I felt bad, but I politely declined. I decided to wait until Miguel got home to see if we had a chance and a future together. I didn't want to get married and wake up one morning next to Sean, wondering if I had made a mistake and if I should have waited for Miguel.

The day finally arrived for Miguel to return from his mission. I waited with a large group of family and friends in the San Jose International Airport to welcome him home. I was both nervous and excited to see him after two long years. We started dating again and in time Miguel told me that he would like to get married within a year. I answered back in a sassy way by saying, "To who?"

What was I so afraid of? What was one of my biggest fears? I was petrified of commitment! Fear has a way of imprisoning you if you allow it to. Fear can keep you on the sidelines of life. This was not my first encounter with intense fear. When I was 16 years old I had a choice to check myself into the prison of fear or to bust out and be free. The location was Yosemite National Park. I was there on a youth adventure trip.

I found myself stuck between a rock and a hard place. The rock was Half Dome and the hard place was my fear of heights. To climb to the top of Half Dome you hold onto cables as you ascend the mountain. As I began my climb, I held onto the cables for dear life and I was downright terrified! At that moment I had a choice to quit or keep climbing. I could give up or go up. I chose to go up. It was not an easy decision, but I chose to crush my fear and keep climbing one shaky step at a time.

My goal wasn't to be the fastest climber. My goal was to make it to the top. It helped that I had friends in front of me and behind me who encouraged me. I learned the importance of surrounding myself with encouraging people. I made it to the top where the feeling of accomplishment was incredible, and the view was breathtaking!

I made my way back down the mountain once again holding onto the cables for dear life. Something interesting happened when I reached the bottom. There were more members of our youth group who hadn't made the climb yet, so I thought to myself, "Why not hike it again?" I had done it once. I could do it again.

My confidence this time was high, and my fear was low. I knew it was something I could do because I had literally just done it. I could help and encourage other climbers because I had experienced it myself. (I'll talk more about the power of encouraging others in the next chapter.)

The hike felt much easier the second time and when I got to the top I celebrated with a signature move of mine just because I could. This fear of heights would present itself again in my life but because I had crushed this fear by climbing Half Dome twice in one day, I would have more confidence to crush it again!

Later in life, I learned a little trick that helped me continue to crush my fear of heights. This trick helped me to successfully climb a high ropes course in Southern California and to zip-line in Honduras. I screamed almost the whole time on the zip-line, but I did it! I digress…. let's get back to the story of Miguel wanting to get married and me wanting to run away.

I don't have room to share all the details in this short story, but in a nutshell, Miguel and I went our separate ways and dated other people. One day I discovered that he was seriously dating a girl and I realized that if I didn't do something, if I didn't commit, I could lose him!

I chose to look in the "true self mirror" and get real with myself. I chose to face my fears. I became very aware that I was allowing my fear of commitment to hold me back from making this important decision in my life. Miguel and I were in love with each other. We were best friends and we brought out the best in each other. I knew that he would be a faithful husband and a devoted father. I had known him for years and I couldn't imagine my life without him.

I arranged to talk to Miguel in person. I told him that I wanted to date again. He had been very patient with me up to this point, but his reply helped me understand that his patience was running low. He told me that he didn't want to date me, he wanted to marry me. Sometimes it's best to make a decision and move in the direction of that decision.

To make a long story short, Miguel broke up with the girl he was dating, proposed to me and I said "yes". I chose to crush my fears and commit. I chose to make a decision and move in the direction of my decision. The interesting thing is that once I decided and we started making plans for our wedding and our married life together, it was amazing how things fell into place. I felt both excited and peaceful about my decision. I love that feeling of excitement and peace when you know you are moving in the right direction, even when you're unsure of all that lies ahead.

Miguel reached his goal of marrying me within the year and I was able to crush my fear. It was truly the best decision I ever made! I'm deeply grateful that I broke out of the prison of fear instead of staying there as a permanent resident.

Maybe your fears don't have anything to do with heights or commitments but I'm sure that they are very real fears for you. Sometimes in life it's important to be very aware and very real with ourselves so we can recognize our fears and crush them. Sometimes it's best to reflect and answer this question. Are you choosing to crush your fears?

Chapter #3

BE ENCOURAGING

Throughout my life I have been given many opportunities to encourage others. One opportunity came while I was a young girl on my neighborhood swim team. This was a team I had been on since I was five years old.

I wasn't the fastest swimmer or the slowest swimmer, but I was one of the loudest swimmers! I would cheer and encourage my Pinehurst Piranha Swim Team like nobody's business. Because I was so obnoxious, I was officially appointed to be the captain of the swim team and was given a shirt to prove it.

As I grew up, I continued to encourage and empower people and I loved it! I encouraged my own two boys as I attended their sporting events and award ceremonies. They were sometimes embarrassed by my loud screams, cowbells, and clappers, but they always knew deep down that I loved them.

For many years my husband and I have been teachers, leaders and mentors for children and teenagers. We have been to countless sporting events such as football games, wrestling matches, soccer games, and track and field meets, to show our love and support for these awesome young people.

I'll never forget the night we attended a track and field meet to support an amazing teenager we knew and loved. She was competing in the high jump event. It was a chilly night and I huddled with my husband in the stands to stay warm. Before she attempted each jump, this precious young woman looked up into the stands to find us. As if on cue, we screamed at the top of our lungs to encourage and support her! The look on her face was priceless. Her parents were unable to make it to that track meet and she appreciated having a fan club. Don't we all need a fan club sometimes?

When I'm not screaming words of encouragement, I can be found writing them! I believe in the power of positive messages. Sometimes I send a message through social media and sometimes I write a handwritten note. I love to bring a smile to someone's face.

I also believe in the power of care packages. I love to surprise people and make their day with a little something that shows up in their mailbox. I don't put anything fancy or expensive in my packages. It's usually just some homemade brownies or cookies with some candy and a handwritten note of encouragement.

Years ago, I sent a care package to a girl from our church while she was away at college. Years later when I posted something on social media about helping my boys settle into their college apartment, this grateful girl wrote the following comment. "I remember when you sent me a care package when I was in the dorms. Your kindness meant a lot to me."

Through the years I have helped encourage high school students to write great things about themselves in their college application essays. I help them brainstorm about their experiences and why they should get into their college of choice. It can be challenging for high school students to identify the experiences and opportunities they could share in their essays. I ask them questions to help them explore their options.

I recently sat down with an amazing high school senior and told her that she would need to put on her "I am awesome" hat. She looked at me with a funny face. I explained that the hat is figurative (though when I teach about conquering your college application, I use a huge and hilarious hat with a sign on it that says, "I am awesome" to drive home the point).

Mind you, the hat isn't the "I am cocky hat" or the "I am better than you are hat". The hat simply helps them to choose to take a moment to reflect on some of the awesome things they have achieved or overcome in their life. We have all achieved and we have all overcome. It's a matter of putting these experiences into writing. I encourage these students to create essays that help them stand out and show the university that they would be crazy not to accept them as part of their student body!

One of the reasons I love helping teenagers see their greatness is because I struggled so much as a teenager to see my own strengths. (I'll share more about this in the next chapter.) I appreciated family, friends, coaches, and leaders who helped me put on my "I am awesome" hat.

We all need encouragement. Sometimes we offer encouragement to others and like a boomerang effect, encouragement comes back to bless us. I remember one day when I was feeling particularly down and in need of encouragement. I didn't know that a tear-jerking message was about to come through my phone.

I noticed that I had a voicemail. As I listened to the voicemail my eyes welled up with tears of gratitude. It was a message from a young woman that I had the privilege of teaching the year before. She was now away at college. In her message she said that I was an awesome teacher and she shared her gratitude and love for me. I usually erase voicemails, but I didn't erase that one. That voicemail was a keeper. That voicemail was a blessing in my life on the exact day I needed it.

Another time that I received a rush of encouragement was in the lobby of my son's college dorm. I heard my name screamed from across the room. An excited young woman came rushing towards me and gave me a huge hug. Not a quick courtesy hug, but the kind of hug that comes from someone who genuinely loves you. This was a young woman I had the privilege of teaching a few years before. I was so happy to see her and by the way she screamed and hugged me, I could tell that she was happy to see me, too.

Through the years I have received some sweet surprises in my mailbox, in my inbox and on my front porch. These surprises have come from sweet people that I have loved and encouraged and like a boomerang effect, they have loved and encouraged me back. Like the handwritten letter that arrived from Colombia, the postcard that appeared from Greece and the e-mail that came from Bolivia. These encouraging messages brought a smile to my face and helped me to know that I had made a difference in a young person's life.

There's nothing like walking outside to a fun surprise on your front porch. Like the inspirational gift and anonymous note of appreciation that were left on the front porch of my home in San Jose, California. I still to this day don't know who left me that sweet surprise but I'm still grateful for it!

I've also had late night visitors who left a surprise for me to find the following morning. It's hard to describe the feeling of walking outside to find your home decorated with countless paper hearts. This has happened to me more than once. I am humbled that others took the time to cut out a gazillion hearts, came to my home late at night while I was asleep and lovingly placed those hearts everywhere. They truly created an amazing and encouraging memory for me.

We all know that there are plenty of discouragers in the world. I choose to be an encourager and I choose to continually surround myself with other encouragers. I believe we can build an awesome army of encouragers! I invite you to join me by answering this simple question. Are you choosing to encourage others?

Chapter #4

BE STRONG

It's easy to focus on our weaknesses and our failures. Have you ever played your customized failure highlight reel over and over in your head? I know I have! Have you ever noticed just how easy it is to find fault with ourselves?

As a young girl, I really struggled to find my strengths. Other people around me seemed to think I was talented but I didn't think I was. I didn't realize that one of my strengths was my sense of humor.

I had several opportunities to audition for plays. I always auditioned for the main part! I wanted the limelight and the role with the most lines! Do you think I got any of those parts? Of course not, and that's okay. The directors recognized my sense of humor and placed me in roles where I could be hilarious and ridiculous on stage, because that's what I was good at!

For "Hansel and Gretel", I tried out for none other than Gretel and I was given the role of the funny witch. For "Cinderella", what part do you think I tried out for? You guessed it, Cinderella. Are you seeing the pattern here?

My younger sister got the role of Cinderella, (that burned a little bit, okay, it burned a lot) but I was given the role of the most dorky and obnoxious of the step sisters with a hilarious solo. More than 20 years after that play, I got a message from a friend on social media about it. She said, "I'll never forget the toilet paper hanging from the back of your dress. You stole the show!" (Note: The toilet paper was hanging from the back of my dress on purpose to ensure that the audience saw my character as a total dork and apparently it worked!)

My sense of humor won me the title of class clown my senior year. What's hilarious is that both of my sisters were voted class clowns of their graduating classes too. Humor ran in our family. I just didn't see it as a strength at the time. It was right in front of me. Everyone else saw it but me. How ironic is that?!

We have a sign in our home that looks like an eye exam chart. However, unlike an eye exam chart that has random letters, this sign contains a powerful message. If you look at the letters long enough, you begin to see the words and the message becomes clear. We love to watch the look on people's faces when they are trying to figure out what the sign says. They squint their eyes and you can tell that the wheels in their mind are turning.

If someone squints and struggles too long, we offer to help them by pointing out the first two words. Once you see the first two words, the rest of the message comes easily. The sign says, "You rarely see what is right in front of you." Isn't that the truth? It can be difficult to see what is right in front of us, especially our strengths, our talents, our gifts.

During one Christmas season many years ago, my younger sister and I asked for special dolls that were very popular in the 80's. I wanted "Strawberry Shortcake" and my sister wanted

"Blueberry Muffin". On Christmas morning we opened our gifts. Mistakenly, my sister was given "Strawberry Shortcake" and I was given "Blueberry Muffin". It was an honest mistake and mix-up. We had been given the wrong gifts, but we were able to switch the dolls and make it right. No harm done.

In life, I believe that we are all given gifts. There are no mix-ups. We are the ones that get mixed up, when we look at other people's gifts and compare ourselves to them. Gifts are meant to be shared, not compared.

Sometimes it takes someone else to help us put on our "gift glasses" to see our gifts, our talents, our strengths. They can help us see what is right in front of us!

I'd like to tell you about someone who helped me put on my "gift glasses" and see that I had the gift of learning another language. It was a gift that I would need to continue to develop and never give up on. I started taking Spanish in 7th grade but my favorite Spanish teacher was the one I had my last three years of high school.

He gave us exercises that helped us to read and write in Spanish. He also gave us fun assignments that helped us interact with each other and encouraged us to speak the language, even if we did it imperfectly.

One day he assigned us to work in small groups to create a commercial in Spanish. Writing and performing a commercial in English would have been hard enough, but the challenge of doing it in another language added a whole other level of complexity.

My group decided to do a commercial about selling mattresses. I'm not sure how we came up with that idea, but we did! We wrote a hilarious skit in Spanish and attempted to perform it without laughing our heads off.

It was through fun experiences like these that my love for the Spanish language grew and my confidence in speaking the language grew as well. During my senior year I took the Spanish AP class and did my best to prepare for the AP test.

You would think that by the time I took the Spanish AP test, I would ace it, right? Wrong! I choked and bombed the test. I didn't earn any college credits and I could have given up on speaking Spanish. I'm glad I didn't. As I thought about my experience I chose to see what was right in front of me. I chose to face the facts.

- Fact #1 - I had failed one test. That test didn't define me.
- Fact #2 - I loved Spanish and I wanted to keep learning it.
- Fact #3 - My Spanish teacher had helped me see through my "gift glasses" that speaking Spanish was one of my gifts and I was not going to let a failed test score tell me otherwise!
- Fact # 4 - I didn't suck at Spanish. I sucked at high-stress, high-pressure, timed tests. I had test-taking anxiety.

I refused to give up on Spanish. I went to college and took a Spanish placement test there. The difference was that this test was not a high-stress, high-pressure, timed test. I scored well on this test which enabled me to earn college credits and advance into higher-level Spanish classes. I confirmed my belief that I didn't suck at Spanish!

During my junior year in college, I lived in a foreign language student residence apartment. It was an on-campus residence with the sole purpose of immersing yourself in your target language. While in the apartment the rules were simple.

We were required to speak Spanish, watch Spanish media, and listen to Spanish music. It was a complete immersion program and it worked for me! I became fluent and am deeply grateful for that opportunity.

I went on to marry an amazing Spanish-speaking man from Chile! He was glad that I didn't give up and that I became fluent in Spanish because that was his parent's native language and I could communicate with them and his mentally-handicapped brother, Luis.

Years later, when our sons were about six and eight years old, we were asked to serve in a Spanish-speaking congregation of our church. I served as the president of the women's organization and was able to use my Spanish to lead meetings, teach lessons, and plan activities. I am thankful that I didn't let a failure get in my way of pursuing what I loved and focusing on one of my strengths.

Each day we have a choice to be strong and to focus on our strengths. It took me years to discover my strengths. That's why I'm so passionate about helping others find their strengths in less time than I found mine. Here's an essential question for you to consider. Are you choosing to focus on your strengths?

Chapter #5

Be Helpful

Do you know someone who has experienced homesick-ness? Do you believe that there is a cure for it? I discovered that the cure for me was reaching out to help others.

During my childhood and teenage years, I grew up in a loving and lively home. My home was my comfort zone and I had no idea just how homesick I would be when I went to college in another state.

Very quickly, after the initial excitement of settling into my dorm, I missed my home, my family, and friends. I had such a hard time adjusting to life in the college dorms that I considered returning home and attending college in the Bay Area.

Instead of moving back home, however, I discovered a key to success and happiness that would help me throughout my life. I reached out to help others. I joined a service club on campus and was involved in so many sweet service projects that helped me to focus on others.

We fed the homeless, helped make gingerbread houses with abused and neglected children, and made birthday cakes for mentally-handicapped adults. We visited people in prison and sang to the elderly in nursing homes.

During my sophomore year of college, I went to a humanitarian service activity that truly changed my life. We watched a video about orphans in Romania. My heart was deeply touched, and tears poured down my face. I wanted to help them. If someone had given me a ticket to Romania that day, I would have boarded the plane and been off! We weren't however, expected to board a plane and fly to Romania.

Instead, we were invited to a large area in the building where they had prepared service projects that we could work on that would be sent to help the children in Romania. I was ready. I learned how to tie quilts and how to crochet in one day! The activity lasted a few hours, but I didn't want it to end.

I volunteered to take unfinished blankets home with me along with quilting frames to set up in my college apartment. Sometimes when my roommates and I needed a break from our crazy homework, we'd gather around the quilting frames to chat and serve.

I truly found joy in serving. It felt so empowering to help others and feel like I was really making a difference. Little did I know that there would be times in my life when I would find myself on the receiving end of service.

The end of service that was humbling for me and outside of my comfort zone. The end of service that my superhero self would tell me that I didn't need. The end of service that would include admitting that I couldn't do it all and that I needed help from others. These were difficult, eye-opening lessons about being on the receiving end of service.

But for now, let's get back to how I continued to fall in love with serving others and how I did my best to help my children fall in love with serving others too.

I was living in Southern California when Disneyland had a very creative and fun promotion going on called "Give a Day, Get a Day". The way it worked was that on a certain day you could go on Disneyland's website to sign up for the program. Once you signed up you would select a service project to do for a day and in return you would get a free ticket to Disneyland for a day. Pretty sweet deal, right?!

Well, apparently thousands of people thought it was a pretty sweet deal too, because on the appointed day to sign up for the program it was almost impossible to get on the website! I tried. My husband tried. My two boys who were eight and ten years old tried to get in. My oldest son, Caleb, was determined! After the rest of us gave up, he kept trying over and over again until he finally got in and was able to sign us up to participate.

We then had a choice of what charity we would help. We found an organization based in Southern California that helped abused and neglected children. They needed us to make blankets. These blankets didn't require any sewing. You simply bought fleece, cut strips on the sides, and tied them. It sounded like the perfect project for our family.

We bought the fabric, made the blankets, and delivered them to the charity. In return and as promised, we were each given a free ticket to Disneyland for the day. We enjoyed serving and making the blankets together and we enjoyed our day at Disneyland together, too!

Service doesn't always come with an immediate reward like a free ticket to Disneyland, but I truly believe that it blesses not only the life of the person receiving the service but also the life of the person giving the service.

Sometimes we have opportunities to be involved in big service projects and other times we can serve in small and simple ways, like taking in a neighbor's trash can, holding the door open for someone, or letting someone go in front of you in line.

Sometimes a service opportunity presents itself to you, like the time our family was shopping in the Los Angeles Fashion District and we came around a corner to find a blind man who was begging for money. My son Trent, who was 15 at the time, gave him a bill that was larger than I expected a teenage boy to part with, especially to a man who couldn't see. That warmed my heart.

Another event that warmed my heart was when my son Caleb, who was 20 at the time, made brownies and wrote a personal note to his hockey coach who was in his 30's and had just lost his wife to cancer.

We must have done something right as parents to help our children discover the joy of reaching out to help others. You can surprise someone and truly make a difference by being helpful. I invite you to consider this meaningful question. Are you choosing to serve others?

Chapter #6

BE OPEN

We all need solutions to the challenges we face. I'm so thankful for solutions like the one we discovered for our colicky baby who cried for hours until my Mom's neighbor gave us a simple solution that worked like a charm! In this chapter, though, I want to talk about a weight loss solution that a friend shared with me.

When I was pregnant with my second son, Trent, I was diagnosed with gestational diabetes. I was put on a strict diet and had to test my blood sugar four times a day and record the results. I was required to report my results to a nurse on a weekly basis. It was not easy, but I stuck to the diet for the health of my baby. After being on that diet for two months I delivered our 9-pound, 10-ounce baby boy and requested that my sweet husband buy me a chocolate milkshake because I wanted some serious sugar!

Trent was such a big baby that at one point he wore the same size diaper (size five) as his 2-year-old brother! We dressed him as a football player for Halloween and he fit the part perfectly. As he started to crawl and walk he slimmed down. It wasn't until years later in middle school that he slowly packed on quite a few pounds and wasn't happy with himself. Kids made fun of him and he was motivated to make a change.

It was around this same time that I was motivated to make a change myself. The change would begin by changing my thinking about diets. For years after my experience with the gestational diabetes diet, I got into a bad habit. Whenever the topic of dieting would come up in conversations, I would tell people that I was only good at dieting when I was doing it for my baby. I said that so many times that I began to believe it.

It was time to change my thinking, so I took a pro-active approach by creating a positive affirmation. I said it every day for months, in an attempt to open my mind to a healthier lifestyle. My affirmation was, "I prepare healthy foods for myself and for my family." This affirmation was completely untrue, but I wanted it to be true and it was about to come true if I was open to a solution!

I was ready. I was truly searching for solutions. The challenge in the dieting world is that are so many solutions and picking the one that will work for you is no easy feat. One night I attended an outdoor youth activity. The kids were zip-lining, swimming, and having a blast! I was over by the food, because I loved food, but ironically, I had a conversation that night that would help me find my dieting answer. A solution was coming, if I was willing to accept it!

The conversation was with my friend. Her husband had recently lost a lot of weight and because I was searching for solutions, and I like to ask questions, I asked her straight up, "How did your husband lose weight?" She proceeded to tell me about a diet program that helped him lose 50 pounds. It was a diet that involved simple food you could buy at most grocery stores and you didn't have to count calories or starve yourself! I was sold.

The activity was on a Wednesday night. I reviewed the diet program the next day, so I could quickly devise a plan. Our family went grocery shopping and we started the diet the following Monday. I don't know what it is about starting diets on Mondays, but it just felt like a clean start and it allowed me to pig out over the weekend before I had to get more disciplined on Monday!

Bingo, it worked! The diet was designed by a doctor and it worked! It wasn't easy, but I saw results quickly. I started to see pounds melting away and inches melting away. Seeing the rapid results made me more motivated to stick to the diet.

My son, Trent, was sticking to it too, and seeing rapid results. We both felt energized, empowered, and downright lighter! I went down four dress sizes and had to purchase a whole new wardrobe (which I didn't cry about).

The diet not only helped us lose weight, but it helped us learn to live a healthier lifestyle. My positive affirmation was now true. I was preparing healthy foods for myself and for my family. Being introduced to this diet years ago began a health quest for me that I'm still pursuing. I have discovered additional health solutions beyond the original diet program because I've been open to them. The more open you are, the more easily you can identify solutions and take action on them.

We all need solutions to the challenges we face. We don't all have the same challenges but we all have challenges. No one makes it through life without hitting some bumps. What's interesting to me is that some bumps feel bigger than others.

Some challenges in life feel like a simple multiple-choice quiz in school. Other challenges feel much heavier, like a comprehensive final exam in your toughest class in college. (In an upcoming chapter I'll share about a three-year span of my life when I felt like I was getting hit with final after final and what I chose to do about it.) But for now, let me ask you this fundamental question. Are you choosing to search for solutions?

Chapter #7

BE PRESENT

Sometimes it takes a big event to shake us up and help us laser focus on what matters most. I've had more than one of those big events in my life. One such event was when I underwent a simple surgery but endured a complicated recovery. I was incapacitated for a long period of time which helped me clearly see what mattered most.

It was December and I began experiencing excruciating pain in my right arm. My right hand was also feeling numb. One day I went to plug something into the wall and couldn't do it. I had a frozen shoulder and I knew this was a problem I could no longer ignore.

Have you ever had a chip on your shoulder? I laugh when I tell people that I had a chip on my shoulder and had it surgically removed! When I went to the orthopedic surgeon, he found that I had calcium deposits (chips) on my shoulder and recommended that I have surgery to remove them. I was not excited for surgery, but I wanted the pain and numbness to go away. I wanted strength back in my arm and to be able to use it every day. I decided on a date for surgery in February.

I vividly remember the time leading up to my surgery and the pressure I put on myself to get so many things done. I wanted to have things set for my family and set for work before my surgery, since I knew I was basically going to be out of commission with my right arm in a huge sling. What I didn't know was just how long my recovery would take. I had no idea what was around the corner for me and the lessons I was about to learn.

After my shoulder surgery I had complications. I had pain. I had spasms. My shoulder would suddenly spasm and flail out of control. It seemed to have a mind of its own! It was wild and unpredictable like an angry bull at a rodeo. I called it my crazy shoulder. I can laugh at it now, but at the time it was not funny.

My recovery from shoulder surgery was more painful than my recovery from my car accident. It was more painful than my recovery from delivering my 9-pound, 10-ounce bouncing baby boy!

I went to countless physical therapy appointments trying to stretch my shoulder and regain my range of motion. Basic things like doing my hair and changing my clothes were difficult. I was like a small child who needed help to do almost everything.

This was very challenging for me. I didn't like bothering my husband or son to help me tie my shoes, open a water bottle, or drive me to yet another physical therapy appointment. They were happy to help. I just needed to get over myself and ask for their help.

I'll never forget the day that I was highly embarrassed to ask for help with a simple task that I found impossible to do on my own. What was the task, you ask? I needed to shave my armpits! I weighed my options.

My son, Caleb, was out of the country serving a mission for our church in Chile. Sheer distance didn't make that a viable option. My teenage son, Trent, was much closer. He was living at home, but I'm sure that shaving his mother's armpits would have been a traumatizing experience for him. One he would wish to forget but never be able to!

If my Mom or sisters lived closer, I know they would have helped me in a heartbeat, but they lived a couple of hours away. I was not going to make them drive a four-hour round trip just to shave my armpits! That was way too much to ask.

Who else was left? My sweet husband, the one that I thought was too nice when we were younger, remember? I sheepishly asked my husband for help and handed him the pink razor. He didn't even flinch. He loved me enough to shave my hairy armpits!

Little by little, as I kept going to physical therapy and doing the exercises they gave me to do at home, my shoulder improved. It got better but not perfect.

I remember attempting to participate in a yoga class several months after my surgery. I remember feeling so silly that I couldn't raise both of my arms above my head. I'm sure that nobody else in the class cared that I couldn't do this simple task, but I did! I felt ridiculous and attempting to do some of the yoga positions just kept reminding me of how limited I was. I stopped going to yoga for a while.

Over time, I finally came to the realization that I might not get the range of motion in my shoulder to 100 percent. I had a choice to make. Pursue perfection or break up with it? I had to ask myself some questions.

What if I could be happy with my range of motion at 90 percent? What if I could focus on the things I could do with my shoulder and not worry about the things I couldn't do? This was not easy because I tend to be a perfectionist. Being a perfectionist in this situation was not helping me. I chose to break up with perfection! It wasn't serving me. It was suffocating me.

My very long recovery was difficult, yet it helped me to slow down and really focus on what matters most. I couldn't do everything, so I started being selective about what I spent my time and energy on. I found myself doing less and learning the art of being present.

What does it mean to be present? To me it means being "all in". It means doing your best to focus on who or what is in front of you. It means eliminating distractions. It means truly being there and nowhere else. Being "all in" is like taking a shower.

Can you imagine taking a shower without being "all in"? Like leaving one leg out of the shower and refusing to wash it? It's a ridiculous thought, right? Yet sometimes we approach life in this ridiculous way.

Instead of being present and "all in" while having a conversation with someone, working on a project or doing anything that matters, we are sometimes only partially in. We are only sort of there. We are allowing distractions to get in the way.

The next time you find yourself doing this, (being partially in instead of "all in") picture yourself showering with one leg in and one leg out like you are doing the hokey-pokey! Smile inside at the silly image in your mind and then focus on being present. Focus on being "all in".

Let's get back to my very slow recovery from surgery that helped me embrace the fact that slowing down can be a good thing. Slowing down has a way of allowing you to retreat, reflect and sometimes re-set the way you do things.

Slowing down helped me to discover a simple new way that I could coach, teach, and train from home. I began a quest to create short and sweet videos for our clients. I could do what I loved to do, and I could do it completely virtually with videos.

This was a game changer for me. I loved teaching in this simple way and our clients loved learning in this way. They no longer had to come to the office to learn from me. They could watch the videos anytime and anywhere, in their pajamas if they wanted to!

Working from home helped me to focus on someone else who mattered most to me, my youngest son, Trent, who was in high school and would shortly be graduating and off to new adventures.

Sometimes it takes a setback to help you retreat, reflect, and re-set your life. I firmly believe, though, that you don't have to experience a major challenge that stops you in your tracks. You can pro-actively answer this very powerful question. Are you choosing to focus on what matters most?

Chapter #8

Be Teachable

I'm a planner, so I like to plan for what's coming. When I married my husband, I knew that I was marrying into his family which consisted of his Mom, Dad, and his mentally-handicapped brother. Luis was born as a healthy baby boy in San Francisco, California, but an incident happened when he was 16 months old that caused brain damage that would affect him for the rest of his life.

I knew that one day when my husband's parents passed away, my husband and I would be taking care of Luis. We decided that one way we could plan ahead and take care of Miguel's family would be to buy a piece of land and build two homes on it. One for us and one for Miguel's family. We could each have our own space but be close enough to help each other.

We were in our early 30's with two young boys at the time and were quite ambitious. My husband and I are both "Type A" personalities so we felt like this was a project we could pursue successfully.

We were fully warned by people about the crazy home building process. We were told a few things:

1) It wouldn't be an easy process.
2) It would cost more than we planned for.
3) We would probably get divorced in the process.

Well, #1 and #2 turned out to be true. It wasn't an easy process and it did cost more than we planned for. Thankfully #3 didn't turn out to be true for us. We not only stayed married, but our marriage became stronger. The home building process taught us to be teachable and willing to learn.

Building anything from the ground up requires an organized system and plan. It also requires a sense of humor and flexible thinking when things don't go according to plan! It was an incredible blessing that we were able to complete the project in nine months from foundation to finish.

During those nine months we learned countless lessons we will never forget. We had so many crazy experiences, which won't fit into this short story, but I'll share a few embarrassing highlights with you.

Have you ever done something and then asked yourself, "What was I thinking?!" Let's just say that we lost thousands of dollars attempting to add an expensive feature to our house. It was a feature that wasn't necessary, but we thought it could be useful and would make us more self-reliant, so we went for it. That was a massive mistake that we learned a massive lesson from!

We also made the mistake of paying a tile guy by the hour who took his sweet time and would have ended up costing more than we budgeted for. Good thing we figured out this wasn't a good idea on the first shower he was working on and we hired someone else to finish our other bathrooms!

We had a septic system contractor give us a bid and then when the job was done he jacked up the price and gave us a big fat bill. I think he thought that we were young and dumb and would just pay it. I never went to law school but let me tell you that I can build a case, present my facts, and negotiate like no tomorrow. I showed that septic system contractor that I wasn't some airhead and that we weren't going to pay his jacked-up price. He had given us a bid and we weren't going to roll over and be taken advantage of.

When someone finds out that we basically built two custom homes from the ground up, at a pretty young age, they are usually surprised, and they sometimes ask, "Would you do it again?" I smile and quickly say "no".

I am grateful that our homes turned out beautifully, but I wouldn't necessarily put myself through that whole hairy process again. Once was enough for me. My husband, on the other hand, is open to it. He's more of the risk-taker between the two of us. He takes risks all the time doing extreme sports like riding dirt bikes and playing ice hockey!

Building a home from the ground up is a risky experience, one he doesn't mind venturing into again. All I know is that if we ever build another custom home somewhere, someday, we'll have an opportunity to apply all the lessons we learned from our first home building adventure.

Life is full of experiences big and small that we can choose to learn from. Throughout your life as you encounter different experiences, you can answer this empowering question. Are you choosing to learn from your experience?

Chapter #9

Be Simple

From a young age I was a classic overachiever, goal setter, and event planner. Funny enough, my initials were G.O. (Gina Ott) and that's what I did! I was constantly going and doing! I loved to set goals, make action plans, and accomplish things. I planned parties, family vacations, and family service projects.

I made a plan to graduate from college in the shortest time possible. Do you know where I created this plan? On a beach in Hawaii while on vacation with my family! They wanted me to relax and enjoy the beach. I did enjoy the beach, I just enjoyed being productive and making a plan while I was there. I ended up graduating with my bachelor's degree in education in 3.5 years, so my beachside goal-setting and planning session paid off!

I also helped my husband plan for and pursue his business degree. Would you like to guess how long it took for him to graduate? Let's just say that it took so many years to graduate that some people thought he had earned his master's degree!

Why on earth did it take him so long to graduate with a bachelor's degree? It was because we decided to start a family and he chose to work full-time and go to school part-time so that I could stay home with our boys. It was a huge sacrifice on his part, a sacrifice I appreciated at the time, but one that I appreciate even more deeply now.

As I got older I planned and hosted wedding showers, baby showers, birthday parties, anniversary celebrations, going away parties, and graduation gatherings. I planned weddings, fundraisers, service projects, Daddy-Daughter events, and Courts of Honor for Eagle Scouts.

While I planned and accomplished a lot of things, through the years I realized that I was driving myself into the ground. I was adding unnecessary stress to my life. I was suffering from "superhero syndrome". Are you an overachiever who drives yourself into the ground attempting to be a superhero too?

When I was a little girl I wanted to be just like a certain superhero. I asked for a popular superhero clothing item for my birthday. I was not a spoiled little girl and I didn't always get what I asked for, but this particular request was granted, and I was more than excited! I wore my new superhero gear with a huge smile on my face!

I eventually grew out of my superhero gear but that was okay because someone gave me a superhero watch. That watch would fit me forever! I kept acting like a superhero by doing too much and driving myself to the point of physical and mental exhaustion. It was time to retire my superhero watch. It was time to slow down and stop acting like I could do it all.

I still wanted to set goals and plan things, but I desperately needed to simplify the process. I needed to be more flexible with my plans and not so rigid. I used to win limbo contests when I was a teenager because my body was so flexible. Now I needed to focus on having a flexible mind - one that could do things in a simpler way, instead of overcomplicating things.

It was around this time when my husband and I were invited to speak to an amazing group of teenagers in our area. I was determined to put into practice my new favorite word, "simple". We chose to do a workshop that would focus on an important skill in life. The important skill was goal setting.

We shared a short and sweet presentation and a simple system the teenagers could use to set a goal that night and take action to achieve it. What good does it do to learn from a class or workshop and then do nothing about it? We wanted to set these teenagers up for success and encourage and support them to take action.

Sometimes you teach a class and you have a memorable time together, but you don't know if anything you say truly "sinks in" and makes a difference. A few months later, a teenager who had attended our workshop let us know we had made a difference and it absolutely made our day!

I was dropping off my son at a youth activity when a young man flagged me down in the parking lot. His face was full of excitement like he had great news to tell me and that he was going to burst if he didn't let it out! I pulled over and rolled down my window. He practically yelled, "I reached my goal!"

The excitement on his face was priceless. He had set a goal using the simple system we taught him at the workshop. He took action and achieved it! I congratulated him, and was so excited for his big accomplishment. I wiped away a few happy tears as I drove away. My simple goal-setting plan had worked and had made a difference in someone's life!

Simplifying isn't just for goal setting or event planning. What aspect of your life would you like to simplify? The next time you find yourself overcomplicating something, be sure to answer this question. Are you choosing to simplify?

Chapter #10

BE STILL

What does it mean to be still? It means to use your pause button. It means that instead of over-reacting or saying something you can't take back, you stop and think before you speak. What a concept, right?!

Can you imagine how amazingly different the world would be if more people used their pause button before blurting out something they might regret?

The words we say are like toothpaste. Once it's out of the tube (or out of our mouth) it can't go back in. We can apologize, but the words might still be remembered by those who heard them and may have been hurt by them. That doesn't mean that we beat ourselves up with the "forgive me not" stick (more about that in the next chapter) but we can pro-actively move forward in our lives and focus on pushing our pause button.

Can you think of moments in your life when pausing would have been helpful? As I mentioned before, I was the class clown in high school. I liked to make people laugh! I thought I was pretty funny one day when I jokingly said something to my Spanish professor that got me sent to the office. I could have prevented this by using my pause button and thinking before speaking.

Sometimes it's best to pause to preserve a relationship. My husband and I had an opportunity to pause or explode one Friday night when we got a call from our teenage son, Trent.

Miguel and I were out on a date when our son called us and told us that he had a fender bender with his friend who was driving in front of him. Thankfully nobody was hurt but he was really worried about how much it was going to cost to repair the car, especially since it was my husband's car!

Trent's car was at the mechanic shop being repaired for the umpteenth time, so we had allowed him to use my husband's Infiniti to go out with his friends that night. In hindsight, that was not our smartest parenting idea.

We came home right away, and I'll never forget what we found him doing when we walked through the door. Any guesses what a 17-year-old boy who had just crashed his Dad's car would be doing while he waited for his parents to come home?

He was cleaning the toilet! Why would he be cleaning the toilet? He knew that it could cost some serious money to repair the damage and we would require him to help with that money. He knew he would be doing extra chores around the house to earn the money.

The fact that Trent was cleaning the toilet and not just moping around when we came home softened our frustration. I'm happy to report that neither of us yelled at him. Trust me, we're not perfect parents, but on this particular night neither of us raised our voices.

We both used our pause button instead of yelling and saying things we would possibly regret later. It wasn't easy because we had enough going on in our lives at the time and we didn't really need a car repair to add to the mix, but we chose to pause instead of screaming at the top of our lungs.

Thankfully and miraculously, there was no damage to the car that Trent had hit. We breathed a huge sigh of relief. Then we had a choice to make. We had two options and two questions to ask ourselves.

- Option #1 - Do we go through insurance, let them pay for the damage, increase our premium and taint our son's driving record?
- Option #2 - Do we let our son pay it off himself and learn a valuable lesson?

We chose Option #2. We took the car to more than one place to get quotes for the repair cost. The repairs were cosmetic repairs, but the unfortunate thing was those cosmetic repairs were going to cost close to $4,000! It was tempting to yell and scream after we got the quotes, but we chose to pause and make a rational plan.

We told our son that he would need to earn $2,000 and then we would pay the other $2,000 to get the car repaired. We figured that he could pay half for his mistake and we would pay half for our mistake of letting him drive our car! Trent did jobs around the house and jobs for our business. He worked and saved and worked and saved.

When he had saved his $2,000, he actually found a much less expensive solution to the car problem while driving around town. I thought it was pure genius of a teenage boy to discover a solution on his own. I'm convinced it's because he was choosing to be open and was searching for solutions.

The cost for his simple solution was $100 instead of $4,000 and completely covered up all of the damage that had been done. You could no longer see that the car had been in an accident. It was like hitting the undo button. It was brilliant!

Years after this experience, Trent sent me a message that made me smile and I'm not going to lie, it made me cry. He said, "I love you so much! You really loved me by teaching me to have skills, not just giving me things."

The night Trent crashed the car was a night that we had a choice to make. It wasn't easy, but I'm very thankful that my husband and I both used our pause button and we preserved the relationship with our son. Using your pause button can help you to preserve important relationships in your life. Are you ready to answer the next question? Are you choosing to use your pause button?

Chapter #11

BE FORGIVING

Do you know someone who constantly beats themselves up for past mistakes? Maybe it's someone you've known for a long time, maybe it's someone you just met or maybe, just maybe, it's you.

It was the day of my youngest son Trent's 8th-grade graduation. I had a handmade poster to wave and cowbells to ring when they called his name to walk across the stage. He was excited to graduate from middle school. He wasn't excited that we were moving the very next day to another city where he would attend a new high school. Our older son wasn't excited either since he was going to be a junior at the same new high school.

Years later when both of my boys were away at college and my husband and I were official empty nesters, I had a chance to reflect. I started to think about the things I could have done to be a better mother.

I was beating myself up with what I call the "forgive me not" stick. Have you ever beaten yourself up with the "forgive me not" stick? At times we can be our own worst enemy. Some sticks can help you, like a walking stick on a long hike. Some sticks can hurt you. This stick was not helping me, it was hurting me. I decided to break up with the "forgive me not" stick and reflect on the good things I had done!

Have you ever made a list of the good you have done? If not, I highly recommend it. Here's a portion of my list.

Let's see... so we didn't raise our children under one roof, but they always had a roof. Yes, that roof changed more times than they liked it to, but they always had a roof. The reason we moved the day after my son's 8th-grade graduation was because we had a better business opportunity that would help us keep a roof not only over our heads, but also over the heads of my husband's family who depended on us for financial support.

My reflection continued. I asked myself an important question to help me focus on the good. The question was, "How have I helped my children?" Here are some of the things I came up with.

- I taught them to work and showed them how to save. I taught them a simple money system that helped them each save more than $10,000 before they turned 18. Earning and saving money were skills that would help them keep a roof over their own heads and the heads of their future family someday.
- I supported both of my boys in earning the rank of Eagle Scout, the highest advancement rank in Scouting.
- I attended their concerts, recitals and talent shows. I nearly froze while supporting them at ice hockey and

roller hockey games, but I was there cheering and encouraging them. I looked like a dork all bundled up in my sleeping bag, blankets, beanie, and jacket but I was there. If awards were being handed out for the loudest Mom, I would have won!

- I helped in their classrooms at school. One time I was questioned at school for teaching second graders a completely innocent Spanish song (from a children's song book from the library, mind you) that one parent thought was inappropriate. Now, that's a good story!

- I joined the running club with my boys in elementary school even though I despised running. For a brief time, we ran every morning before school. Thankfully my children lost interest in the running club and since I was never interested in the running club in the first place, except to support them, I encouraged them to pursue other exercise options!

- I helped them set goals and get into their college of choice. When they were young I took them on a personal tour of the university that I graduated from. They could see and feel how amazing the campus was. They both worked hard, got better GPA's than I did, and were accepted to the same school!

- I gave them opportunities to serve and help others. Sometimes we participated in large organized service projects like planting trees for our community or collecting canned food for the local food bank. Sometimes we did simple things like making loaves of "Pumpkin Chocolate Chip Bread" or "Banana Oatmeal Chocolate Chip Cookies" and delivering them to friends and neighbors. Can you tell that our family loves chocolate? Our friends and neighbors love it too!

I'll be the first to admit that I've never been the perfect parent, but my kids knew I loved them, and I honestly did the best I could.

None of us is perfect. What we all have in common is that we all make mistakes. We can apologize for those mistakes, do our best to make them right, and then we have two options.

- Option #1 – Keep beating ourselves up.
- Option #2 – Forgive ourselves.

Which option do you choose? I invite you to think deeply about this question. Are you choosing to forgive yourself?

Chapter #12

Be Thankful

"Thank you so much for teaching me the importance of gratitude. I will never forget it."

"I don't know if you realize what a difference you made to a class of 16-18-year-olds those two years you taught us. You taught me about gratitude, about loving others...."

These are real messages from real teenagers who I had the privilege of teaching for two years in a daily early morning scripture study class. Why would they thank me for teaching them about gratitude? Let me explain.

Every morning before school started, we met together to study the scriptures. Every morning at o'dark thirty I stood in front of these tired teenagers (my oldest son, Caleb, being one of them) attempting to engage their interest and teach them a thing or two. One thing I wanted to teach them was the art of being grateful.

Each morning, at the beginning of class, we spent about five minutes writing down what we were thankful for in simple composition notebooks. I called them our "blessing journals". I put on some soft music and we wrote away - myself included! There's something really powerful about starting your day in gratitude and thanksgiving. After we finished writing, I would ask if anyone wanted to share what they wrote with the class.

My students were juniors when we started doing this daily gratitude exercise. I grew to love the teenagers in this class so much that I requested to teach them again during their senior year. My request was granted. Guess what we kept doing their senior year? You got it, blessings journals!

For two years we focused on gratitude every day. For two years we started our day in thanksgiving. For two years they may not have learned anything else from me, but they learned the art of being grateful!

When they graduated, I gave each of them a new blessing journal and encouraged them to continue writing in it each day. I wrote a personal message in the front of each of their journals. I wrote about the greatness I saw in them and how thankful I was to be their teacher. Teaching that class was a blessing for me. Our daily gratitude exercise blessed my life as well as theirs.

Those two years of focusing on my blessings and writing daily in my blessing journal were preparing me for a difficult time that was coming in my life when my husband and I would have multiple health problems. I would need to keep writing in my blessing journal and keep pulling out my "gratitude glasses" to look for the good in my crazy life! The rest of this chapter is written from a place that might surprise you. Here goes...

I'm writing this part of the chapter in the waiting room of a surgery center. I don't mind waiting anywhere as long as I have books to read and a place to write. Today writing takes my mind off the surgery room and worrying about my husband. Writing is a tool of positive distraction for me.

Why would I be writing about gratitude in the waiting room of a surgery center? Because I'm choosing to focus on my blessings. In our home we have a sign that reads, "There is always, always, always something to be thankful for" and I believe this to be true with all my heart! Through every challenge in my life, I have discovered that focusing on my blessings helps me remain positive, helps me remember the big picture, and helps me be downright happier!

In a span of less than three years, my husband and I have had six surgeries between us. The first two surgeries were mine. They were both oral surgeries for my magnificent mouth that was originally botched up at age 14 in my car accident and was still causing problems!

Next was a shoulder surgery for my husband's left shoulder. A few months later was a shoulder surgery for my right shoulder. Then my husband had emergency gallbladder surgery and finally today's surgery is on my husband's right shoulder. Don't even get me started on why we needed all of these surgeries. Let's get to the thankful part!

I choose to be thankful that in all of these surgeries we have had skilled surgeons and clean facilities. I choose to be thankful for the family and friends who reached out and helped us in so many ways. They prayed for us, brought delicious meals to our home, sent us notes, texts and love. Being on the receiving end of service was humbling and hard for me but I was deeply thankful for every hand that reached out to help me and my family.

I'm thankful for the handwritten messages of encouragement the 14-year-olds in my Sunday school class sent me after my shoulder surgery. I still have those messages and treasure them today.

I'm thankful for sweet friends who came to visit one day bearing gifts of yogurt, homemade granola, and strawberries from the juiciest strawberry stand in the county. I was in the fetal position in pain while they visited me, but their love and kindness warmed my heart. I devoured the sweet treats after they left and only shared a little bit with my family!

I'm thankful that we were home when my husband needed emergency gallbladder surgery and that one of the best surgeons in California was on call at the hospital we rushed to. If my husband's attack had happened one week earlier when we were in a remote location on a dirt biking trip, it would have been difficult, expensive, and stressful to get him to the nearest emergency room, possibly by helicopter!

My husband's surgeon was amazing, and my husband's case was off the charts. He was an overachiever in making gallstones. The ultrasound tech had never seen that many gallstones show up on the screen in his life. The "Most Gallstones Award" is not an award anyone really wants to win!

I'm thankful that we were safe while driving home in the pouring rain from my husband's first shoulder surgery when someone hydroplaned in front of us and boomeranged across the freeway. That was quite an experience and quite a story.

I'm thankful that five months after my shoulder surgery I could share my experiences about my recovery and my gratitude for my blessings. I had the opportunity to be a motivational speaker and team-building activity leader at a youth camp on Catalina Island. I spoke about my crazy shoulder recovery and about remaining in gratitude no matter what!

I also shared a gratitude game with them that they could play anywhere, anytime, in their mind! I played it on the boat ride over to Catalina, so I would stay distracted, since I was feeling seriously seasick and didn't want to throw up.

I'm thankful that a simple shiny penny reminds me every day to be thankful. Have you been wondering when I was going to introduce the penny? Keep reading and you'll see how a simple penny can be the key for inviting thankfulness into your life and living from a place of gratitude.

In this case, the penny has nothing to do with money. The penny simply serves as a reminder to be thankful every day. The more we focus on being thankful, the happier we truly are. The penny is part of a daily challenge. It's one of the simplest challenges that helps you to live in gratitude every day.

Wouldn't it be incredible if more people were thankful every day? We can't control how thankful others are, just like we can't control other people's pause buttons, but we can choose to live in gratitude ourselves! Let me ask you this question. Are you choosing to be thankful?

Chapter #13

Accept the Challenge

The challenge is to begin each day in gratitude and thanksgiving.

Step #1
The first step is to find a penny. Go ahead and put the book down if you need to go search for one. I don't mind waiting.

Step #2
Now that you have the penny, place it face down in a location close to your bed. It's best to have it in a place that will be in front of your face when you wake up (like on your nightstand).

Step #3
Each morning when you see the penny, make a conscious choice to begin your day in gratitude. Once you do, turn the penny over so the face side is up. It's your way of congratulating yourself on facing the day with gratitude!

You may ask, "How will I express my gratitude each day?" You can express it in more than one way. The choice is yours. You can say a prayer of gratitude or you can play the gratitude game. Do you remember the game I said I played on the boat ride over to Catalina Island, so I wouldn't get sick?

It truly is a game you can play anywhere, anytime, in your mind. You simply think "I'm thankful for _______________" and fill in the blank. The boat ride over to Catalina was so long that I probably filled in that blank more than 100 times!

You also have the option to keep a written record of your gratitude (like the blessing journals that my students and I wrote in each morning). One thing that is really powerful about keeping a written record (whether it's a physical journal or a digital one) is that you can look back and be reminded of the blessings in your life.

My students and I faithfully wrote in our journals each morning and from time to time we would do a blessing journal review. I would give the class five minutes to review the things they had written in their blessing journals and would then allow them to share any insights or feelings they had about their experience. It was powerful to see these amazing teenagers look back and use their own written record to remember blessings that otherwise could have been easily forgotten.

It's been years since I taught those sweet students, but I still keep a blessing journal and from time to time I choose to do my own blessing journal review. My record helps me remember what my mind can quickly forget.

Each day you decide how you will express your gratitude. Each night you repeat step #2 of the challenge and each morning you repeat step #3. Before you know it, this gratitude practice can become a positive habit in your life. You might even find that what you start in the morning continues throughout your day. It's like starting the day by putting on your "gratitude glasses" and never taking them off.

If you stick with it, you may find that you are living in gratitude so often that it is becoming your general mindset or way of thinking. This is a great place to be and it takes continual practice. I like to call it "gratitude mindset practice". Funny enough, the acronym for "gratitude mindset practice" happens to be GMP. These same letters happen to be my initials (Gina Margaret Pomar).

I wasn't born with a gratitude mindset though. I've chosen to practice it through the years, even during some of my most difficult challenges. I'm determined to continue practicing it every day for the rest of my life. Will you join me? Will you accept the challenge?

Chapter #14

TAKE ACTION

Congratulations! You made it to the final chapter. As you know, it's easy to start reading a book. It's not always easy to finish one, so give yourself a nice little pat on the back. I know the book title mentions 12 questions, but I'm going to throw some more questions your way because I can!

How many times have you read a book, loved it, and done nothing about it? As I mentioned in the beginning of the book, I've done that more times than I can count, and I wanted to write a book that was different. You've read this book, I sincerely hope you've loved it, and I invite you to do something about it! What can you do, you ask? Here are some ideas to help you get started.

- <u>Stay connected</u> - Go to www.ginapomar.com
- <u>Start the challenge</u> - Find a penny and begin tonight. You can do it!

Last question, I promise.... sometimes I just can't help myself! Who do you know that would love this book and love you for sharing it with them?

- <u>Share the book</u> - Make a difference in someone's life!

Meet the Author

Hello there, Gina here. If you've read this book, you've met me through my hilarious and heart-warming stories. (Hopefully you think they are as hilarious and heart-warming as I do!) These stories are just the tip of the iceberg when it comes to my crazy life.

Are you wondering what's next? Visit me online to see what I'm working on…

www.ginapomar.com

Until next time…